T0084819

THE PRESIDENCY OF

Franklin D. ROOSEVELT

CONFRONTING THE GREAT DEPRESSION AND WORLD WAR II

BY DON NARDO

CONTENT CONSULTANT
GLEN JEANSONNE
PROFESSOR, DEPARTMENT OF HISTORY
UNIVERSITY OF WISCONSIN—MILWAUKEE

COMPASS POINT BOOKS
a capstone imprint

Compass Point Books are published by Capstone,
1710 Roe Crest Drive, North Mankato, Minnesota 56003
www.capstonepub.com

Copyright © 2015 by Compass Point Books, a Capstone imprint.
All rights reserved. No part of this publication may be reproduced in whole or
in part, or stored in a retrieval system, or transmitted in any form or by any
means, electronic, mechanical, photocopying, recording, or otherwise, without
written permission of the publisher.

Editorial Credits
Melissa York, editor; Becky Daum, designer; Maggie Villaume, production
specialist; Catherine Neitge and Ashlee Suker, consulting editor and designer

Image Credits
AP Images, 35, 43; Corbis: 31, 39, 50, 52, Bettmann, 11, 12, 15, 18, 23, 25,
26, 28, Hulton-Deutsch Collection, 17; Franklin D. Roosevelt Presidential
Library and Museum, 57 (bottom); Getty Images: AFP, cover; Library of
Congress, 5, 7, 8, 21, 31, 36, 41, 48, 57 (top); National Archives, 47; Red Line
Editorial, 40; Thinkstock: Tetra Images, 55; U.S. Marine Corps, 45
Art Elements: Shutterstock Images

Library of Congress Cataloging-in-Publication Data
Nardo, Don, 1947–
   The presidency of Franklin Roosevelt : confronting the Great Depression and
World War II / Don Nardo.
       pages cm.—(Greatest U.S. presidents)
   Includes bibliographical references and index.
   ISBN 978-0-7565-4927-5 (library binding)
   ISBN 978-0-7565-4935-0 (paperback)
   ISBN 978-0-7565-4943-5 (ebook PDF)
1. Roosevelt, Franklin D. (Franklin Delano), 1882–1945—Juvenile literature.
2. Presidents—United States—Biography—Juvenile literature. 3. United States—
Politics and government—1933-1945—Juvenile literature. I. Title.
   E807.N26 2015
   973.917092—dc23   [B]   2014007422

Printed in Canada.
032014   008086FRF14

TABLE OF CONTENTS

Chapter One

THE BRINK OF COLLAPSE

4

Chapter Two

THE HISTORIC HUNDRED DAYS

14

Chapter Three

AMERICA'S NEW DEAL

24

Chapter Four

DEFENDER OF DEMOCRACY

34

Chapter Five

ORDEAL OF TOTAL WAR

44

Timeline 58

Glossary 60

Additional Resources 61

Source Notes 62

Select Bibliography 63

Index 64

The Brink
OF COLLAPSE

Franklin Delano Roosevelt knew he was stepping into one
of the worst crises in U.S. history. Taking office as president
March 4, 1933, one of his paramount jobs was to reassure
Americans they could get through the tough economic times.
Addressing the nation at his inauguration, he projected courage,
saying, "Let me assert my firm belief that the only thing we
have to fear is fear itself." That fear, he said, was a "nameless,
unreasoning, unjustified terror which paralyzes needed efforts
to convert retreat into advance." In other dark hours of the

Franklin Delano Roosevelt (right) rode to his first inauguration with the previous president, Herbert Hoover.

nation's history, he said, its leaders had spoken frankly to Americans. This was because their support was "essential to victory." Roosevelt called on his fellow citizens to support him now, "in these critical days."

Several of the words the new president had chosen clearly described a serious, grim, and even dire situation. Yet he was not exaggerating when he used such terms as "fear," "terror," "dark hour," and "critical days." As he delivered the speech at the U.S. Capitol in Washington, D.C., the country was in deep trouble. The United States and most of the rest of the world had fallen into the worst financial slump of modern times. It became known to history as the Great Depression.

This frightening, menacing state of affairs had reached a tipping point three years earlier. Trading on the New York Stock Exchange seemed strong the morning of Monday, October 21, 1929. This was no surprise to stockbrokers. They felt positive about the future because the U.S. economy appeared very healthy. And they believed the enormous bubble of prosperity that had grown during the 1920s would continue to expand.

But during the afternoon of October 21, the country's massive financial bubble began to burst. Stock prices suddenly fell at a startling, frightening pace. Surprised brokers hoped it was a temporary fluke. But it was not. There were problems throughout the world economy. U.S. farms had been losing money throughout the 1920s. And Europe had never fully recovered economically from World War I (1914–1918).

The situation worsened, and within a few days the stock market had lost a record $14 billion. It took another terrible hit on October 29, losing $15 billion. That brought losses for a period of less than two weeks to $50 billion. (This equals many hundreds of billions in today's money.)

Crowds gathered outside the New York Stock Exchange as word of the crash spread.

In the United States, many people who had seen themselves as rich, or at least comfortable, were suddenly almost flat broke. With little or no money to spend, millions of people stopped buying things. Most people purchased only essentials. Faced with plummeting sales, stores started laying off clerks and other employees. Hard-hit stores ordered fewer products from manufacturers. With their orders swiftly dropping, factories became the next domino to fall. Some fired many or most of their workers, while others shut down entirely, never to open their doors again.

Meanwhile, the huge numbers of workers fired from stores and factories swelled the ranks of jobless Americans. The national unemployment rate had been a low 3 percent before the October 1929 stock market crash. But by the early months of 1930, that rate stood at 9 percent. And when Roosevelt entered the White House in March 1933, by some estimates 25 percent of Americans were out of work.

Poverty deepened for many families that were already poor before the Great Depression.

Some of the jobless turned to their savings accounts to make ends meet. But for millions of people this was no longer an option. By the early months of 1933, more than 9,000 U.S. banks had gone bankrupt. When they closed their doors, all of the money the banks had been holding for their customers effectively disappeared. In a tragic instant, millions of Americans lost their life savings. One minute they had been secure and hopeful. In the next they were penniless.

IT'S A FACT

According to government estimates, 26,355 U.S. businesses failed in 1930, the first full year of the Depression. Even more—28,285—went out of business the following year.

The Great Depression changed the lives and futures of large numbers of Americans in negative ways. As a result the country underwent drastic and in some ways permanent changes. This made the crippling financial crisis "one of the turning points of American history," in the words of historian William Leuchtenburg. Thus, when Roosevelt took office as president, one major era of U.S. history ended, and another was just beginning.

It is difficult for most modern Americans to imagine the hardship and desperation faced by ordinary people during the

LETTER OF HARDSHIP

The extent and severity of the Depression caused hardships for millions of individuals and families. Their stories convey the dark times more vividly than any statistic could. One such story was that of a 17-year-old girl from Buffalo, New York. In desperation she wrote to first lady Eleanor Roosevelt, who was a tireless advocate for the needs of women and the poor. "I heard that you have been very good to the poor," the note begins. "I am writing this letter to see if you can help me. I had to leave school because I didn't have any clothes to wear. I will be very thankful to you if you can gather some clothes [for me]. My father is working and making a little money but we are barely living ... All I am asking for is a few dresses and a winter coat. Thank you for anything you can do."

Great Depression. Yet this was the awful shape the country was in when Franklin Delano Roosevelt, often called simply FDR for short, delivered that first inaugural speech. The question in everyone's minds was whether he could make things better. Could he succeed in pulling the nation back from the brink of collapse?

One of those present seemed to have no doubts on that account—Roosevelt himself. "We must act and act quickly," he told the citizens gathered at the Capitol. "I assume unhesitatingly the leadership of this great army of our people dedicated to a disciplined attack upon our common problems." He also promised to "wage a war against the emergency, as great as the power that would be given to me if we were

Roosevelt (center) entered the White House with wife Eleanor and son James confident he could tackle the nation's problems.

in fact invaded by a foreign foe." That bold pledge to attack the Depression as if the country were at war was no empty statement. The world was about to witness a great leader awaken a sleeping giant—the hidden and untapped energies and creativity of an equally great people.

TRIUMPH IN ADVERSITY

Franklin Delano Roosevelt was born January 30, 1882, in Hyde Park, New York. He was the son of well-to-do, socially prominent parents— James Roosevelt and Sara Delano Roosevelt. Young Franklin received an excellent education. In addition to having private tutors, he attended first-class private schools. He earned a degree in history from Harvard University and studied law at Columbia University. In 1905 he married his distant cousin, Anna Eleanor Roosevelt, who was the niece of President Theodore Roosevelt. Franklin and Eleanor had six children, one of whom died in infancy.

For a while Franklin Roosevelt practiced law in New York. But in 1910 he entered politics. A member of the Democratic Party, he was elected to the state senate. Three years later President Woodrow Wilson appointed him assistant secretary of the U.S. Navy. Roosevelt served in that capacity until 1920, gaining valuable military knowledge he would later use as commander in chief.

Roosevelt was stricken with polio in 1921, which left him unable to walk and using a wheelchair. Yet he courageously fought his way back into politics and was elected governor of New York in 1928. Not long afterward he began campaigning for president. He boldly asserted that he could fight the Depression more effectively than President Herbert Hoover. The American people agreed, electing Roosevelt as the nation's 32nd president in a landslide victory in November 1932. Taking office a few months later, he initiated the now famous collection of federal programs known as the New Deal.

Later, after the United States entered World War II in 1941, Roosevelt helped other Allied leaders defeat the Axis powers—Germany, Italy, and Japan. In all, he served three full terms and part of a fourth, longer than any other president. He died April 12, 1945, at age 63. Historians are nearly unanimous in viewing him as one of the most important and influential national leaders of the 20th century.

Chapter Two

The Historic
HUNDRED DAYS

The stock market crash and Great Depression began not long after Herbert Hoover, Roosevelt's Republican predecessor, became president. So Hoover and his administration had the first opportunity to combat the enormous financial crisis. But when Hoover left office early in 1933, the Depression had an even stronger grip on the country than it had in 1929.

Hoover and his advisers supported the idea of private charities helping society's poorest individuals. But they strongly felt that the federal government should not operate in any way

Homeless people around the country built makeshift villages of shacks many people called "Hoovervilles."

like a charity. Instead, Hoover said, the most effective approach was to rely on Americans to help themselves. They should work as diligently as possible. And then if they still needed help, they could turn to private charities and other local relief efforts.

Later in his term, Hoover supported some government programs to combat the Depression. Indeed, Hoover intervened more than previous presidents had during economic troubles. But the Depression continued to worsen, and as it did, Hoover became increasingly unpopular. In the 1932 presidential campaign, Roosevelt wisely capitalized on the sitting president's economic troubles. Roosevelt argued that private charities and local state and town relief efforts were not the answer to the problem. These groups were simply not up to the task. The ravages of the Depression were gigantic, he said, affecting tens of millions of people. So the resources of charities and local relief groups had rapidly been exhausted.

During the campaign Roosevelt insisted that the only way out of the current crisis was for the federal government to step in. Moreover it must act on a very large scale. He said this was the only way to lessen the suffering of millions of desperately poor people. In a radio address in April 1932, Roosevelt pledged to help "the forgotten man at the bottom of the economic pyramid." His government would begin large-scale programs to fight poverty. Yet poor people would not be the sole focus of his activist policies. "I pledge you," he stated the following July, "I pledge myself, to a new deal for the American people."

These two words—*new deal*—quickly came to describe Roosevelt's government policies and programs. The New Deal was "a happy phrase," major Roosevelt supporter and the president's secretary of labor Frances Perkins later said. "It made people feel better, and in that terrible period of depression they needed to feel better." Americans responded to the promise of the New Deal in droves. On election night

Roosevelt traveled through rural Georgia during his 1932 campaign and talked with farmers about the Depression.

in November 1932, Roosevelt won overwhelmingly. Roosevelt scored 472 electoral votes, which came from 42 of the 48 existing states. That left Hoover only 59 electoral votes from six states.

Once in office as president, Roosevelt wasted no time in beginning the policies he had promised in the campaign. The roughly three months that followed his inaugural address in early March 1933 later came to be called the Hundred Days. They turned out to be historic—the new president and his Democrat-controlled Congress accomplished so much at what many people called blinding speed.

A group of expert advisers known as the Brain Trust helped craft new programs and laws. Under Roosevelt's lead Congress passed one sweeping legislative bill after another. And for the most part, the country backed this full attack on the Depression. Never before or since did a U.S. president enjoy the support of so many varied groups of Americans, from unions and organized labor, to small farmers and urban workers, to women and African-Americans.

Roosevelt's opening move against the crisis was to restore confidence in American banks. Thousands of them had closed and most of the ones still open were in disarray. Just two days

Stabilizing the financial industry would help prevent bank runs, in which worried crowds of customers tried to withdraw their money at the same time.

after taking office, on March 6, 1933, the president initiated a national bank holiday. Every operating bank in the country had to close temporarily. U.S. Treasury officials then inspected their books to find out which ones were most in need of help. Only when a bank's finances were sound would it be allowed to reopen.

Three days later, on March 9, the Emergency Banking Act came before Congress. It gave the federal government more power to intervene during the crisis. Congress passed it and Roosevelt signed it into law within hours. This was one of the fastest passages of federal legislation in U.S. history. "We do not want and will not have another epidemic of bank failures," the president told the American people. He kept this promise. In short order the banking crisis ended, and millions of people began to feel their faith in the system restored. "We seem to be off to a good start," Roosevelt told a friend.

His words turned out to be an understatement. On the heels of the bank holiday came one far-reaching federal program after another. For example, before Roosevelt's first months in office were over, two major programs were up and running— the Agricultural Adjustment Administration and the Civilian Conservation Corps. The AAA was designed to increase poor farmers' profits. It called for them to produce fewer livestock and less grain, rice, and other crops. In theory this would make the goods scarcer. And because they were in shorter supply, the goods would be more valuable and their prices would go up. This would allow the farmers to make more money.

The Civilian Conservation Corps (CCC) was intended to put unemployed young men from 18 to 25 years old back to work. These jobs did not only provide the men employment. They also improved the country and the quality of life of its citizens. Projects included planting trees, fighting forest fires, building dams, improving parks and trails, and other similar jobs. Between 1933 and 1941, the CCC employed more than 2 million people.

Among the other programs created during the Hundred Days was the Federal Emergency Relief Administration. It gave money to individual states and local agencies to run work projects. A common example was putting up new buildings on public lands. Meanwhile, the Tennessee Valley Authority (TVA) paid tens of thousands

IT'S A FACT

A national poll taken in April 1936 showed that 82 percent of Americans supported the CCC because it provided work for millions of young men who would otherwise be jobless.

of people to build more than a dozen large-scale dams in the Tennessee River Valley. In addition to providing jobs, the TVA dams furnished millions of Americans with cheap electricity.

Posters encouraged young men to join the CCC.

PLANNING FOR THE FUTURE

One of the most important concepts that the new president introduced in his first term was that the nation must do a better job of planning for future growth and possible major crises. The message rings clear in an excerpt from his April 10, 1933, speech about the Tennessee Valley Authority.

The TVA, he said, "should be charged with the broadest duty of planning for the proper use, conservation and development of the natural resources of the Tennessee River ... Many hard lessons have taught us the human waste that results from lack of planning. Here and there a few wise cities and counties have looked ahead and planned. But our Nation has 'just grown.' It is time to extend planning to a wider field ... This in a true sense is a return to the spirit and vision of the pioneer. If we are successful here we can march on, step by step, in a like development of other great natural territorial units within our borders."

Still another program instituted in the period was referred to as the Truth-in-Securities Act. It reformed the stock market, making future crashes less likely.

In only a few months, the daring and eager new president changed the way the U.S. government worked. Gone was the reserved approach of public officials reluctant to step in. Roosevelt and members of his political party seemed ready to try almost anything to get the economy moving. And most Americans responded positively. They generally agreed that some of the new programs might not work. But at least the government was making a real effort. Most people "couldn't understand these things that were being passed so fast," key

Roosevelt adviser Raymond Moley later admitted. Yet "they

knew something was happening, something good for them."

Also, they knew who was making that something happen.

They listened to Roosevelt speak on the radio, explaining his

programs and why they were important. And they liked what

they heard.

Roosevelt worked with Secretary of the Interior Harold L. Ickes (center) and Secretary of Agriculture Henry A. Wallace (right) to create and promote many New Deal programs.

Chapter Three

America's NEW DEAL

The flurry of political activity that occurred during the Hundred Days stunned the country. The federal government created new programs and initiatives at a dizzying pace. And through it all, Franklin Delano Roosevelt remained firmly at the government's helm, captain of a ship of state still foundering in a dangerous financial storm.

There were, to be sure, people who did not like or trust the new president. Some political conservatives were sure he would ruin the country. He would create a giant welfare state, they

Roosevelt signed the Banking Act of 1933 (also called the Glass-Steagall Act) on June 16, 1933, at the end of the Hundred Days. Among other banking system reforms, the act limited some of the activities of commercial banks.

warned, making people dependent on government handouts. Most Americans, however, supported Roosevelt and his new, bold policies.

Roosevelt's personal attributes helped gain the public's trust as well. Though he had been in office only a few months, he had already displayed several of the qualities that made him a remarkable politician and leader.

Roosevelt was extremely likable and projected a caring, fatherly image. "He was so confident and charismatic," a scholar wrote. "He spoke so eloquently and with such compassion" that Americans "trusted him unreservedly."

Roosevelt was also a master of timing. "He understood when to invoke the prestige of the presidency," says historian Doris Kearns Goodwin. He also knew "when to hold it in reserve, when to move forward, and when to pull back." Roosevelt recognized this quality in himself, as Goodwin notes, saying, "I am like a cat. I make a quick stroke and then I relax."

Roosevelt spoke to crowds in Atlanta, Georgia, in support of the New Deal in 1935.

Clearly, the new president felt his first year or two in office was the time to make that quick stroke and move the nation forward. In his first three months he had gotten more done than many former presidents had in an entire four-year term. But considering the terrible crisis the country was in, even that much was not enough for Roosevelt. In the months and years that followed, he continued his grand political experiment.

That experiment was the New Deal. It consisted of combating the Depression with every new and daring idea Roosevelt and his advisers, often called "New Dealers," could conceive of. They readily admitted they were sailing through largely unknown waters. The nation had never before been in such economic troubles. Therefore, they believed, it was necessary to take a hit-or-miss approach. The result was that some New Deal programs were very successful. Others were only somewhat successful. And still others were failures.

Of the New Deal programs that worked well, some were so successful that they survive today. Probably the most familiar example is Social Security. Passed in August 1935, the Social Security Act was designed to provide financial aid to society's most vulnerable citizens. These included the elderly, jobless, and chronically ill.

Secretary of Labor Frances Perkins was instrumental
in the success of the Social Security Act.

Under the plan Roosevelt signed into law, both employees and their bosses contribute to Social Security funds on a regular basis. The Social Security Administration then sends money from the funds to those who are older than 65, out of work, or too sick to work, with some qualifications and exceptions that have changed over the years.

At the time the act first passed, Roosevelt admitted, "We can never insure one hundred percent of the population against one hundred percent of the hazards ... of life." Nevertheless, he added, "we have tried to frame a law which will give some measure of protection to the average citizen." In particular, it would help to protect people faced with "poverty-ridden old age."

Roosevelt's political opponents were squarely against Social Security. They warned it would promote un-American values. Republican senator Daniel O. Hastings of Delaware was one. "I fear it may end the progress of a great country," he said.

But Roosevelt and his supporters remained firm in their faith that Social Security would work, both then and in the future. Ever since its passage, Social Security has been one of the most popular of all federal programs.

Another widely admired program Roosevelt's administration created in his first term was the Public Works Administration (PWA). The president assigned his secretary of the interior, Harold L. Ickes, to lead it. The PWA created jobs by making agreements with private contractors. These

IT'S A FACT

U.S. Secretary of Labor Frances Perkins argued that Social Security would help make future depressions less likely. She said: "It will make this great republic a better and a happier place in which to live— for us, our children and our children's children." Perkins was the first woman to hold a position in a president's Cabinet.

builders constructed schools, hospitals, dams, tunnels, roads, sewage systems, and other sorts of public works. The scope of the PWA's accomplishments was huge. It employed half a million people each year. And in the eight years it existed, it encompassed more than 34,000 projects. Some, including Washington State's Grand Coulee Dam and New York City's Lincoln Tunnel, were immense undertakings.

Another New Deal program was the Works Progress Administration (WPA). Similar to the PWA, it employed people in projects meant to benefit all Americans. Begun in the spring of 1935, and overseen by New Dealer Harry Hopkins, it grew to be the largest of all the programs Roosevelt created. This

THE WPA

In some ways the WPA resembled the PWA. Both programs built bridges, roads, and airport runways, for example, as well as parks, city halls, and libraries. But in addition the WPA sponsored arts-related projects, including the Federal Music Project, the Federal Writer's Project, and the Federal Theater Project. These and other similar programs produced hundreds of thousands of music concerts, stage shows, and museum exhibits. Sooner or later a majority of Americans attended at least one of the presentations. More than 40,000 artists were hired to create murals and other art. "Some of it was good," Roosevelt remarked, and "some of it not so good, but all of it native, human, eager, and alive: All of it painted in their own country, and painted about things that they know and look at often and have touched and loved."

Charles Wells' New Deal murals, a WPA project, hang in the Clarkson S. Fisher Federal Building and U.S. Courthouse in Trenton, New Jersey.

fact can be seen in the sheer number of people it employed—roughly 8.5 million.

To help revive industry, Roosevelt introduced the National Industrial Recovery Act in his first year in office. The agency that would carry out this legislation was called the National Recovery Administration. The NRA strove to restore competition in the marketplace; to aid factory and business owners in planning; and to improve jobsite conditions for workers. Lawmakers hoped that meeting these and other objectives would help businesses to be more productive. In turn this would stimulate the economy. The program's main tool was an extensive series of regulations that kept wages and prices fixed at certain levels.

The NRA's goals turned out to be overly optimistic, however. Economists and historians continue to debate the degree to which those goals were met. Many American companies did not like the idea of the government setting prices and wages, and the Supreme Court agreed. In 1935 it declared the NRA unconstitutional, saying it had over-regulated commerce. Still there is general agreement that the program helped many demoralized Americans feel better.

Modern experts find it difficult to judge how effective the New Deal was overall. This is largely because Roosevelt's original plans for recovery never reached completion. In 1939 World War II erupted in Europe. European production was disrupted, and U.S. industry increased in order to fill Europe's needs. In time the United States was drawn into the conflict. And most New Deal programs were replaced by a surge of war production and military jobs.

For Roosevelt the war posed a major new challenge. He had earlier faced and battled the Great Depression as if he were a general in wartime. Now he faced a situation in which he was indeed the nation's commander in chief in a real military conflict. He sensed that this, his second enormous undertaking as president, would test his stamina, resolve, and abilities as a leader. Moreover, with U.S. enemies seeking world domination, for him failure was simply not an option.

Newspapers poked fun at Roosevelt's many programs, often popularly referred to as alphabet soup.

Chapter Four

Defender of
DEMOCRACY

During his first term and part of his second as president,
Franklin Delano Roosevelt spent much of his time tending to
domestic affairs. This was understandable. After all, the Great
Depression held the nation in a devastating grip. Putting jobless
people back to work was a major presidential priority.

The United States had become increasingly isolationist.
Back in the 1800s, the nation had frequently and vigorously
expanded its influence around the globe. But by the early 1900s,
most Americans were more reluctant to get involved in the

Roosevelt began his second term January 20, 1937.

affairs of faraway lands. The large numbers of American soldiers killed in World War I strengthened that attitude. Moreover, between 1935 and 1937 Congress passed a series of so-called neutrality laws. They were intended to keep the country out of foreign wars.

Yet the president could not and did not completely ignore foreign affairs. Roosevelt signed a series of treaties with countries in the Western Hemisphere. Among others, they included El Salvador, Haiti, Brazil, Costa Rica, and Cuba. This Good Neighbor Policy continued previous president Herbert Hoover's diplomatic actions in the region.

The agreements established new, valuable trade relations between those countries and the United States. The treaties

also dealt with important security issues for all involved.
First, there was the issue of the United States being the most
powerful country in the hemisphere. Some fear existed among
its neighbors that it might misuse its great power. But Roosevelt
assured the smaller U.S. neighbors that his nation would not
intrude into their local affairs as it had at times in the past.

The Good Neighbor Policy was formally stated in December
1933. "No state has the right," it went, "to intervene in the
internal or external affairs of another." Furthermore, Roosevelt

The WPA published materials supporting the Good Neighbor Policy.

said, the United States was the world's leading democracy. So it would work diligently to help the Latin American countries strengthen their own democracies.

Roosevelt also pledged that the U.S. would protect the neighboring states from menacing overseas powers. During the 1930s potential trouble was brewing abroad. Germany, led by dictator Adolf Hitler, was arming itself at an alarming rate. Japan was doing the same, threatening the peace of East Asia. Many of the Latin American states worried they might become targets of German or Japanese aggression. Roosevelt told them that a U.S. umbrella of protection would prevent that from happening.

Yet Roosevelt saw that promising to protect America's neighbors from aggressors was not enough in those troubled times. He worried about what would happen if those same aggressors attacked the United States. He watched as a number of ominous events occurred on the global stage in the mid-1930s. In 1936 Hitler placed large numbers of troops near the border between Germany and one of the world's leading democracies, France. This was clearly a threat to French security.

Even more worrying, in 1937 Japan launched a massive invasion of China. Part of ongoing Japanese expansion, the island nation's goal was to seize East Asia's vast and valuable farmlands and other natural resources. Soon Japan joined the equally warlike Germany and Italy, creating the Axis powers.

Roosevelt viewed the growing militarism of the Axis as a serious threat to world peace and democracy. "The peace, the freedom, and the security of 90 percent of the population of the world is being jeopardized by the remaining 10 percent," he said in 1937. The Axis powers, he added, "are threatening a breakdown of all international order and law."

Roosevelt and the country did not want war. But the president correctly recognized that Germany and Japan were bent on unlimited expansion. He feared they were after world domination. If so, he realized, the United States would not be able to sit on the sidelines of what was likely to be a bloody war. In his now famous Quarantine speech, delivered in Chicago in October 1937, he stated his belief that the "disease" of war was spreading and it was up to "peace-loving" nations to quarantine the growing violence.

Roosevelt's fears were proven accurate when Hitler invaded Austria in March 1938. The United Kingdom, France, the United States, and the other leading democracies had warned Germany not to do so. Such a move would be unacceptable, they had

The aggression and growing military force of Adolf Hitler (left) threatened Europe by the end of the 1930s.

said. Yet when Austria fell, the United Kingdom and France did nothing. And swayed by the isolationist forces in its midst, the United States followed their example. Although Hitler claimed that Austria would be his last territorial demand, Roosevelt did not believe it. He told a friend it was dangerous for the world that no one was calling the Axis nations' bluffs.

Roosevelt soon found one of his worst fears transformed into reality. In September 1939 Hitler's armies marched into

ALLIED AND AXIS POWERS IN WORLD WAR II, DECEMBER 1939

■ Allied Powers

■ Soviet

□ Neutral

■ Axis Powers

Italy joined the Axis in June 1940. The Soviets joined the Allies in June 1941. The United States joined the Allies in December 1941. Parts of China were under Axis control throughout the war.

Poland. Because the United Kingdom and France had promised to come to Poland's aid, the attack ignited World War II.

Although the United States was not yet in the conflict, Roosevelt reasoned that the chances were high the country would have to take part sooner or later. It depended on how well the French and the British did against the German war machine.

To many people around the world, the Germans seemed unstoppable. France fell to Hitler's forces in June 1940. And Hitler mounted a monstrous air assault on southern England in August 1940.

AT THE POINT OF A GUN

President Roosevelt gave 30 speeches over the radio between 1933 and 1944. These Fireside Chats were intended to reassure the American people and explain his policies. Roosevelt made it clear to his fellow Americans in a December 29, 1940, radio address that Germany and the other Axis powers were a serious threat to the United States.

"If Great Britain goes down," he said, "the Axis powers will control the continents of Europe, Asia, Africa, Australia, and the high seas—and they will be in a position to bring enormous military and naval resources against this hemisphere. It is no exaggeration to say that all of us, in all the Americas, would be living at the point of a gun ... Some of us like to believe that even if Britain falls, we are still safe, because of the broad expanse of the Atlantic and of the Pacific. But the width of those oceans is not what it was in the days of clipper ships."

Roosevelt's Fireside Chats helped the country understand the president's policies during the Depression and World War II.

It was clear to Roosevelt that his own country must do whatever was necessary, short of sending troops and directly intervening in the war, to help the British. In a radio speech delivered in late December 1940, he explained to the American people why the nation "must be the great arsenal of democracy." He pointed out that aiding the United Kingdom and its allies now would help the United States later. A strong, unconquered United Kingdom would stand as a barrier between Hitler's Europe and the Americas. "The people of Europe who are defending themselves do not ask us to do their fighting," he declared. "They ask us for the implements of war, the planes, the tanks, the guns, the freighters which will enable them to fight for their liberty and for our security." He strongly asserted, "We must get these weapons to them."

Roosevelt's proposed program to send arms and other supplies to the besieged British was called Lend-Lease. It began early in 1941. By the end of the war, it had given away

IT'S A FACT

Great Britain was the primary recipient of the arms, food, and other supplies given away by the Lend-Lease program. But the United States also lent such supplies to several former and current British colonies in the British Commonwealth, the Soviet Union, China, Brazil, and others, for a total of more than 40 nations.

Roosevelt and Winston Churchill (right) discussing the Atlantic Charter

guns, ammunition, tanks, warplanes, trucks, food, and other supplies worth almost $51 billion.

British prime minister Winston Churchill and Roosevelt soon became friends as well as colleagues in the fight to save the world from Axis domination. They met aboard a ship near Newfoundland, Canada, in August 1941. There they drew up the Atlantic Charter. The crucial agreement cemented the U.S.-British alliance, making it stronger than ever. In the document the two nations stated that together they would defend free, democratic peoples everywhere against aggression. Together with the Good Neighbor Policy and Lend-Lease program, the charter established Roosevelt as one of the world's leading defenders of democracy.

Ordeal of
TOTAL WAR

The war-production programs Franklin Delano Roosevelt

had pushed for to help the British and other nations at war with

the Axis powers were not his only acts of military preparedness.

He was well aware that his own country might be pulled into the

widening conflict. So it seemed wise to him to begin preparing

for such a situation. In June 1940 he signed into law a naval

expansion act passed by Congress. Its main purpose was to

build a two-ocean navy in case the nation found itself at war

with Germany and Japan. The following September Congress

The Japanese attack on Hawaii's Pearl Harbor propelled the U.S. into the war.

and Roosevelt created the first peacetime conscription in U.S. history. Approximately 800,000 men were drafted into the armed forces.

The country began preparations with no time to spare. On December 7, 1941, the Japanese launched a sneak attack on the U.S. naval base at Pearl Harbor, in Hawaii. More than 2,000 Americans were killed and the U.S. Pacific fleet was badly damaged.

Reaction from Americans was almost unanimous. Outraged, people across the country called for the president to strike back against Japan. And he did so. The next day—December 8—Roosevelt asked for a declaration of war from a packed joint session of Congress.

With an expression of grim determination, he called December 7 "a date which will live in infamy." Japan had "deliberately sought to deceive the United States by false statements and expressions of hope for continued peace." Yet it attacked Pearl Harbor, as well as other military bases belonging to U.S. allies. The president then assured his listeners that "no matter how long it may take us to overcome this premeditated invasion, the American people in their righteous might will win through to absolute victory."

Winston Churchill received a written copy of the speech not long afterward. Since 1939 he and other British leaders had yearned for the United States to enter the conflict on their side. The world was engulfed in an ordeal of total war, with the very future of freedom and democracy at stake. Churchill was certain that U.S. industrial might and war production would be enormous and prove to be a virtually unstoppable force. He later noted, "To have the United States at our side was to

PROPOSED MESSAGE TO THE CONGRESS

Yesterday, December 7, 1941, a date which will live in ~~world history~~ *infamy*

the United States of America was ~~simultaneously~~ *suddenly* and deliberately attacked

by naval and air forces of the Empire of Japan.

The United States was at the moment at peace with that nation and was *still in* ~~continuing the~~ conversations with its Government and its Emperor looking

toward the maintenance of peace in the Pacific. Indeed, one hour after

Japanese air squadrons had commenced bombing in *Oahu* ~~Hawaii and the Philippines~~,

the Japanese Ambassador to the United States and his colleague delivered

to the Secretary of State a formal reply to a ~~former~~ *recent American* message. ~~from the~~

~~Secretary.~~ *While* This reply ~~contained a statement~~ *stated* *it seemed useless* that diplomatic negotiations

~~must be considered at an end, but~~ *it* contained no threat ~~and no~~ hint of *an* *or war*

armed attack.

It will be recorded that the distance ~~of Manila and especially~~ of

Hawaii, from Japan make it obvious that the attack ~~were~~ *was* deliberately

planned many days ago. *or even weeks* During the intervening time the Japanese Govern-

First draft of "Day of Infamy" speech with Roosevelt's notes

me the greatest joy ... Hitler's fate was sealed. [Italian leader]

Mussolini's fate was sealed. And as for the Japanese, they

would be ground to powder. All the rest was merely the proper

application of overwhelming force."

Women entered the workforce in high numbers, helping increase industrial output.

Churchill was glad for another reason. Namely, a major
part of that "proper application" of force would now rest in the
hands of the most talented and worthy leader he knew. He was
sure that Roosevelt would be a first-rate commander in chief.
And this proved to be the case. Roosevelt set in motion the

largest burst of war production the world had ever witnessed. Many factories never closed. They ran 24 hours a day, seven days a week, producing staggering amounts of weapons, food, clothes, and other goods.

The result was beyond impressive. A mere year after the attack on Pearl Harbor, U.S. war production equaled the entire industrial output of Germany, Japan, and Italy combined. And in the months and years that followed, America's output came to dwarf that of the Axis nations. American workers built thousands of warships each year. U.S. farmers produced hundreds of millions of tons of foodstuffs.

Roosevelt also increased the efficiency of U.S. war efforts by pushing Congress to pass a number of crucial measures. One of these set up a system of rationing. Civilians were allowed to purchase only limited amounts of certain products. They included gasoline, tires, shoes, beef, coffee, and sugar. Thanks to this system, American soldiers had better access to the goods they required to achieve victory. Roosevelt also instigated a 48-hour workweek

IT'S A FACT

U.S. war production under Roosevelt was enormous. Between 1942 and 1945, the military machine he oversaw created more than 17 million rifles, 87,000 tanks, and 296,000 planes.

for critical American workers. In many sectors this was eight hours more than it had been before the war.

These and other actions Roosevelt took demonstrated two of his many leadership abilities. One was an ability to focus like a laser beam on the needs of the present. As Doris Kearns

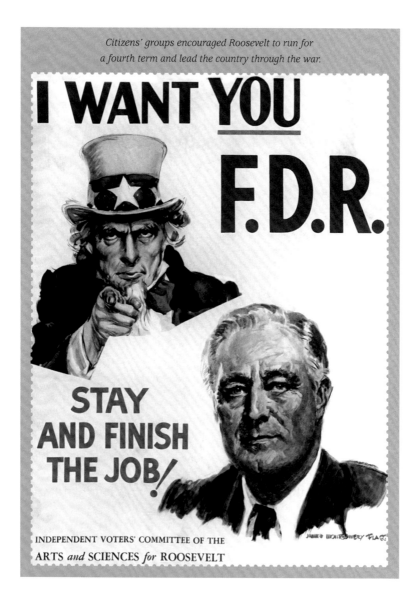

Citizens' groups encouraged Roosevelt to run for a fourth term and lead the country through the war.

Goodwin points out, he was able "to close his mind against the setbacks of the past and focus instead on making plans."

Another of Roosevelt's leadership strengths was a broad understanding of the various interest groups and opposing forces within American society. This gave him helpful insights into how to unify them. "No one understood better than he,"

IT'S A FACT

During World War II, Roosevelt signed an executive order requiring many Americans of Japanese descent to leave their homes and live in internment camps in remote areas. The government believed these people were sabotaging the war effort or spying. Today the internment of Japanese-Americans is considered unjust and motivated by racism rather than any military need. The government has apologized and paid reparations for its actions.

author Eric Larrabee wrote, "the inner dynamics of American strength." Roosevelt grasped "how to mobilize it, how to draw on it, how to gauge its limits. Once mobilized," he realized, "it did not need to be driven. It needed only to be steered."

Americans viewed Roosevelt as such an effective leader that they kept re-electing him. As the war in Europe and Asia ground on, he gained a third term in 1940 and then his fourth in 1944. By the time that fourth term officially began in 1945, the Axis powers were on the verge of total defeat.

Roosevelt rarely allowed himself to be photographed in a wheelchair.

But Roosevelt would not serve out his entire fourth term. Nor would he have the chance to witness the great victory he helped ensure.

During his years in the White House he had borne the crushing weight of the presidency. And fighting both the Depression and a world war had taken an awful toll on him. The strain of his huge workload as president had prematurely aged him, as has happened to many U.S. presidents. He grew increasingly weak and prone to colds and bronchitis, and by

1944 his doctors insisted he should work no longer than four hours a day.

Eventually, it appears, Roosevelt's body simply could take no more. He was working in the study of his presidential retreat in Warm Springs, Georgia, early in the afternoon of April 12, 1945. Shortly after the butler entered to serve him lunch, the president's body suddenly lurched. "I have a terrific pain in the back of my head," Roosevelt exclaimed. Those were his last words. He collapsed and never regained consciousness, falling to a massive stroke.

Across the free world immediate reactions to Roosevelt's death were shock and deep sadness. There was an unspoken realization that the nation, as well as the world, had lost someone of epic stature. U.S. senator Robert Taft summed up how most people felt when he said that Roosevelt's passing "removed the greatest figure of our time at the very climax of his career." The loss, Taft continued, "shocks the world to which his words and actions were more important than those of any other man. He dies a hero of the war, for he literally worked himself to death in the service of the American people."

At the time most people recognized Roosevelt as an unusually effective leader. Over time historians came to confirm

THE BRITISH FOREVER THANKFUL

Americans were not the only ones saddened by the news of Roosevelt's passing April 12, 1945. In the United Kingdom, Winston Churchill spoke for himself and his countrymen. He publicly recognized that to some degree they owed their survival as a people and a nation to that recently deceased American president. Without the Lend-Lease program and other aid that Roosevelt had poured into Great Britain, Hitler's Germans may well have overrun the British Isles. Churchill recalled "the valiant and magnanimous deeds of the USA" under Roosevelt's guidance. Those actions, he said, "will forever stir the hearts of Britons in all quarters of the world in which they dwell."

that judgment, as well as elevate him to the rank of one of the top presidents. This assessment is based on his striking list of achievements in the office.

He mobilized the demoralized American people at the height of the Great Depression. The New Deal, by itself, did not completely restore the economy. That was accomplished by the tremendous surge of war production in the early 1940s. Yet Roosevelt's domestic programs lifted Americans' spirits, turning them away from fear and defeatism.

In a very real way, Roosevelt put the U.S. back on its feet. He also guided it away from isolationism. These feats made it possible for the nation to lead the world to ultimate victory over the Axis powers. In addition, he coined the term *United Nations*, and in his final year as president he helped to create that important international body dedicated to fostering peace and cooperation among the world's nations.

Through the years of turmoil, Roosevelt quite literally reinvented the U.S. government. He did this by thrusting it into areas in which it previously had little or no involvement. These included reforming financial institutions, working conditions, and loan programs for farmers and homeowners; protecting

Roosevelt was integral in the creation of the United Nations, which has its headquarters in New York City.

the environment; and helping the elderly and poor through Social Security.

Roosevelt also expanded the importance and reach of the president. Under his leadership the chief executive came to have more prestige and power than ever before. He created numerous new government agencies under the control of the executive branch; pushed through many large-scale programs, such as Social Security, that affected millions of Americans; extended more governmental power over the economy; and greatly expanded the military, over which the president is the supreme commander. In this and other ways, he "re-created the modern presidency," as historian Leuchtenburg put it. Roosevelt's biographer Ted Morgan went even further. "He transformed America," he said of Roosevelt. "The country we are living in today is to a great extent of his making." His tools were a sharp political mind, a magnetic personality, and immense courage. Using them, a man who could not walk taught a great people how to run toward and take charge of the future.

TIMELINE

1882
Franklin Delano Roosevelt is born January 30 into a wealthy, socially prominent family in Hyde Park, New York

1910
After working as a lawyer, Roosevelt enters politics, running for New York state senator

1932
Roosevelt campaigns for president and in November defeats the sitting president, Herbert Hoover, in a landslide victory

1933
Roosevelt is inaugurated as the 32nd president and immediately launches the New Deal, a huge legislative attack on the Depression; in his first 100 days in office, the Civilian Conservation Corps, Agricultural Adjustment Administration, Tennessee Valley Authority, and other large-scale programs designed to reverse the financial downturn begin operation

1939
Roosevelt worries about the security of Great Britain and France after Hitler orders his troops to invade Poland, igniting World War II

1940
France falls to German forces; Roosevelt is re-elected to a third term as president

1928
Roosevelt is elected governor of New York

1921
Roosevelt contracts polio, and afterward uses a wheelchair for the rest of his life

1929
The New York stock market crashes and the economy spirals downward

1935
Roosevelt signs the Social Security Act, which creates a system to financially aid elderly and poor people

1936
Roosevelt is re-elected to a second term as president

1941
Roosevelt launches the Lend-Lease program, which sends weapons and supplies to aid Great Britain and other U.S. allies; Japanese air and naval forces attack the U.S. naval base at Pearl Harbor, in Hawaii; Congress declares war on Japan and Germany

1944
Roosevelt is re-elected to a fourth term as president

1945
Roosevelt dies April 12 in Warm Springs, Georgia

GLOSSARY

bankrupt—unable to pay debts

bronchitis—an illness of the throat and lungs

charismatic—charming

chief executive—another term for the president of a country

demoralized—very discouraged or depressed

inaugural address—a speech given by a new president on the day he or she takes office

isolationism—a point of view that holds that a nation should take care only of itself and stay out of the affairs of other countries

magnanimous—generous

optimistic—hopeful and positive about the future

polio—short form of the word poliomyelitis, a disease that may cause paralysis

stockbroker—a person who buys and sells stocks and other financial commodities on the stock market

vulnerable—open to being hurt or exploited by someone else

ADDITIONAL RESOURCES

FURTHER READING

Bolden, Tonya. *FDR's Alphabet Soup: New Deal America, 1932-1939.* New York: Alfred A. Knopf, 2010.

Doak, Robin S. *Black Tuesday: Prelude to the Great Depression.* Minneapolis: Compass Point Books, 2008.

Reis, Ronald A. *The Great Depression and the New Deal: America's Economy in Crisis.* New York: Chelsea House, 2011.

INTERNET SITES

Use FactHound to find Internet sites related to this book. All of the sites on FactHound have been researched by our staff.

Here's all you do:

Visit *www.facthound.com*

Type in this code: 9780756549275

CRITICAL THINKING USING THE COMMON CORE

Franklin Delano Roosevelt is admired for his inspirational speeches. Choose a quote from one of Roosevelt's speeches. What effect do you think Roosevelt was trying to achieve from the quote? How do you think Roosevelt's listeners received the quote? How does the quote make you feel? (Craft and Structure)

Roosevelt did not get involved in World War II until U.S. soil was attacked, even though U.S. allies were already at war. How do you think things might have turned out differently if the country had entered World War II earlier or later? (Integration of Knowledge and Ideas)

Every previous president followed the example of George Washington by stepping away from the presidency after two terms. Why do you think Roosevelt broke this precedent? Why do you think Americans elected him four times? (Key Ideas and Details)

SOURCE NOTES

Page 4, line 6: Franklin Delano Roosevelt. "First Inaugural Address." The Miller Center University of Virginia. 3 March 2014. http://millercenter.org/president/speeches/detail/3280

Page 9, line 16: William E. Leuchtenburg. *Franklin D. Roosevelt and the New Deal, 1932-1940.* New York: Harper and Row, 1963, p. xv.

Page 10, sidebar, line 12: Richard Cohen, ed. *Dear Mrs. Roosevelt: Letters from Children of the Great Depression.* Chapel Hill: University of North Carolina Press, 2002, p. 52.

Page 10, line 8: "First Inaugural Address."

Page 16, line 11: Samuel I. Rosenman, ed. *The Public Papers and Addresses of Franklin D. Roosevelt.* New York, Random House, 1938, vol. 1, p. 625.

Page 16, line 14: Ibid., p. 659.

Page 16, line 18: Frances Perkins. *The Roosevelt I Knew.* New York: Penguin Books, 2011, p. 166.

Page 19, line 11: *The Public Papers and Addresses of Franklin D. Roosevelt,* vol. 2, p. 63.

Page 19, line 15: Elliott Roosevelt, ed. *FDR: His Personal Letters, 1928-1945.* New York: Duell, Sloan, and Pearce, 1950, p. 338.

Page 22, sidebar, line 11: *The Public Papers and Addresses of Franklin D. Roosevelt,* vol. 2, pp. 122-123.

Page 22, line 11: Studs Terkel. *Hard Times: An Oral History of the Great Depression.* New York: New Press, 2000, p. 250.

Page 25, line 9: Adam Cohen. *Nothing to Fear: FDR's Inner Circle and the Hundred Days That Created Modern America.* New York: Penguin, 2009, p. 4.

Page 26, line 1: Doris Kearns Goodwin. *No Ordinary Time: Franklin and Eleanor Roosevelt: The Home Front in World War II.* New York: Simon and Schuster, 1994, p. 608.

Page 28, line 7: *The Public Papers and Addresses of Franklin D. Roosevelt,* vol. 4, p. 324.

Page 29, line 8: Samuel Eliot Morison, Harry Steele Commager, and William E. Leuchtenburg. *The Growth of the American Republic,* vol. 2. New York: Oxford University Press, 1980, p. 506.

Page 29, sidebar, line 5: William Leuchtenburg, ed. *The New Deal: A Documentary History.* New York: Harper and Row, 1968, p. 86.

Page 30, sidebar, line 19: Jean Edward Smith. *FDR.* New York: Random House, 2007, p. 356.

Page 36, line 8: Ibid., p. 115.

Page 38, line 5: Franklin Delano Roosevelt. "Quarantine Speech." The Miller Center University of Virginia. 3 March 2014. http://millercenter.org/president/speeches/detail/3310

Page 38, line 16: Ibid.

Page 41, line 7: Franklin Delano Roosevelt. "Fireside Chat 16: The Arsenal of Democracy." The Miller Center University of Virginia. 3 March 2014. http://millercenter.org/president/speeches/detail/3319

Page 42, line 5: Ibid.

Page 46, line 7: Franklin Delano Roosevelt. "Address to Congress Requesting a Declaration of War." The Miller Center University of Virginia. 3 March 2014. http://millercenter.org/president/speeches/detail/3324

Page 46, line 22: Winston Churchill. *The Second World War.* vol. 3, Boston: Houghton Mifflin, 1950, p. 539.

Page 51, line 2: *No Ordinary Time,* p. 294.

Page 51, line 12: Eric Larrabee. *Commander in Chief: Franklin Delano Roosevelt, His Lieutenants, and Their War.* Annapolis: Naval Institute Press, 2004, p. 11.

Page 53, line 7: *No Ordinary Time,* p. 602.

Page 53, line 16: Ibid., p. 606.

Page 54, sidebar, line 16: *The Second World War,* vol. 6, p. 476.

Page 56, line 11: *Franklin D. Roosevelt and the New Deal, 1932-1940,* p. 327.

Page 56, line 13: Ted Morgan. *FDR: A Biography.* New York: Simon and Schuster, 1985, p. 772.

SELECT BIBLIOGRAPHY

Badger, Anthony J. *FDR: The First Hundred Days*. New York: Hill and Wang, 2008.

Badger, Anthony J. *The New Deal: The Depression Years, 1933–1940*. New York: Farrar, Straus and Giroux, 1989.

Black, Conrad. *Franklin Delano Roosevelt: Champion of Freedom*. New York: Public Affairs, 2003.

Brands, H. W. *Traitor to His Class: The Privileged Life and Radical Presidency of Franklin Delano Roosevelt*. New York: Doubleday, 2008.

Churchill, Winston, and Franklin Delano Roosevelt. "Atlantic Charter." Yale Law School: The Avalon Project. http://avalon.law.yale.edu/wwii/atlantic.asp

Cohen, Adam. *Nothing to Fear: FDR's Inner Circle and the Hundred Days That Created Modern America*. New York: Penguin Press, 2009.

Cohen, Richard, ed. *Dear Mrs. Roosevelt: Letters from Children of the Great Depression*. Chapel Hill: University of North Carolina Press, 2002.

"Franklin D. Roosevelt Presidential Library and Museum." http://www.fdrlibrary.marist.edu/

Goodwin, Doris Kearns. *No Ordinary Time: Franklin and Eleanor Roosevelt: The Home Front in World War II*. New York: Simon and Schuster, 1994.

Johnson, Gerald W. *Franklin D. Roosevelt: Portrait of a Great Man*. New York: W. Morrow, 1967.

Kennedy, David M. *Freedom from Fear: The American People in Depression and War, 1929–1945*. New York: Oxford University Press, 1999.

Larrabee, Eric. *Commander in Chief: Franklin Delano Roosevelt, His Lieutenants, and Their War*. Annapolis, Md.: Naval Institute Press, 2004.

Leuchtenburg, William. *Franklin D. Roosevelt and the New Deal, 1932–1940*. New York: Harper and Row, 1963.

Leuchtenburg, William E., editor. *The New Deal: A Documentary History*. New York: Harper and Row, 1968.

McElvaine, Robert. *The Great Depression: America 1929–1941*. New York: Times Books, 1993.

Morgan, Ted. *FDR: A Biography*. New York: Simon and Schuster, 1985.

Olson, Lynne. *Those Angry Days: Roosevelt, Lindbergh, and America's Fight over World War II, 1939–1941*. New York: Random House, 2013.

Perkins, Frances. *The Roosevelt I Knew*. New York: Penguin Books, 2011.

Persico, Joseph E. *Roosevelt's Centurions: FDR and the Commanders He Led to Victory in World War II*. New York: Random House, 2013.

"Presidential Speech Archive." The Miller Center University of Virginia. http://millercenter.org/president/speeches#fdroosevelt

Rosenman, Samuel I. *The Public Papers and Addresses of Franklin D. Roosevelt*. New York: Random House, 1938.

Schlesinger, Arthur M., Jr. *The Coming of the New Deal*. Boston: Houghton Mifflin, 2003.

Shlaes, Amity. *The Forgotten Man: A New History of the Great Depression*. New York: HarperCollins, 2007.

Smith, Jean Edward. *FDR*. New York: Random House, 2007.

Watkins, T. H. *The Great Depression: America in the 1930s*. Boston: Little, Brown, 1993.

Weintraub, Stanley. *Final Victory: FDR's Extraordinary World War II Presidential Campaign*. Philadelphia: Da Capo Press, 2012.

INDEX

Agricultural Adjustment Administration (AAA), 19–20
Atlantic Charter, 43

banks, 9, 18–19
Brain Trust, 18

Churchill, Winston, 43, 46–47, 48, 54
Civilian Conservation Corps (CCC), 19–20

Emergency Banking Act, 19
executive power, 55–56

Federal Emergency Relief Administration, 20
Fireside Chats, 41
France, 37–40

Germany, 13, 37–40, 41, 44, 49, 54
Good Neighbor Policy, 35–36, 43
Great Depression, 6–11, 13, 14–18, 32, 34
    hardships, 7–10
    stock market crash, 6, 8, 14, 22
    unemployment, 8–9, 20

Hitler, Adolf, 37–40, 42, 47, 54
Hoover, Herbert, 13, 14–15, 17, 35
Hopkins, Harry, 30
Hundred Days, 17–23, 24

Ickes, Harold L., 29
isolationism, 34, 39, 54

Japan, 13, 37–38, 44–47, 49, 51

Lend-Lease, 42–43, 54

Moley, Raymond, 23

National Recovery Administration (NRA), 31–32
New Deal, 13, 16, 27–32, 54

Pearl Harbor, Hawaii, 45–46, 49
Perkins, Frances, 16, 29
Public Works Administration (PWA), 29–30

Roosevelt, Eleanor, 10, 12
Roosevelt, Franklin Delano
    advisers, 18, 23, 27
    birth, 12
    campaigns, 13, 15–17
    children, 12
    criticisms, 24–25, 29, 32
    death, 13, 53
    disability, 13, 52, 56
    education, 12
    elections, 13, 16–17, 51
    governor, 13
    inaugurations, 4–5, 10, 17

    leadership, 10–11, 13, 25, 33, 48, 50–51, 53–56
    legacy, 13, 53–56
    marriage, 12
    personality, 25–26, 50–51, 56
    radio, 16, 23, 41, 42

    speeches, 4–5, 10, 16, 22, 38, 41, 42, 46
Social Security Act, 27–29, 56

Tennessee Valley Authority (TVA), 20–21, 22
Truth-in-Securities Act, 22

United Kingdom, 38–40, 41, 42–43, 44, 46, 54
United Nations, 54–55

World War I, 6, 35
World War II, 13, 32, 40, 42–43, 44–51, 52
    Japanese-American internment, 51
    military preparedness, 44–45
    rationing, 49
    war production, 32, 42, 44, 46, 49–50, 54
Works Progress Administration (WPA), 30–31

ABOUT THE AUTHOR

Historian and award-winning author Don Nardo has written many books for young people about history, including biographies of presidents Thomas Jefferson and Franklin D. Roosevelt. Nardo lives with his wife, Christine, in Massachusetts.